The Crackdown on Humanitarian Aid in Turkey

MAY 2024

silencedturkey

REPORT BY
ADVOCATES OF SILENCED TURKEY

EDITORS
YOUSEF HARVEY
HAFZA GIRDAP

DESIGN AND ILLUSTRATIONS
MUHSIN NAZIF

CONTRIBUTIONS BY
DENIZ KENAN
MURAT KAVAL

ADVOCATES OF SILENCED TURKEY

AST is a 501(c)(3) tax exempt, not for profit charitable and educational organization based in New Jersey, USA exclusively for defending human and civil rights.

ISBN: 9798325765797

CONTACT
271 US 46, #F 203 Fairfield, NJ, 07004
help@silencedturkey.org

WEB & SOCIAL MEDIA
www.silencedturkey.org
@silencedturkey
facebook.com/silencedturkey
youtube.com/advocatesofsilencedturkey

Copyright © AST Publishing, 2024

All publication rights of this work belong to the Advocates of Silenced Turkey Inc. and AST Publishing. All rights reserved. No part of this book may be reproduced or transmitted in any form or by any means, electronic or mechanical, including photocopying, recording or by any information storage and retrieval system without permission in writing from the Advocates of Silenced Turkey Inc.

CONTENTS

EXECUTIVE SUMMARY	4
INTRODUCTION	5
Objective	6
Methodology	6
The Social Genocide in Numbers	6
Cultural and Social Annihilation	7
The Crackdown's Reach to Samaritans	8
Legal and Social Implications	8
SILENCING COMPASSION: SYSTEMATIC CRACKDOWNS ON PHILANTHROPIC ENDEAVORS	10
Case 1: The Tragic Death of Halime Gülsu in Custody	12
Case 2: The Persecution of Nihat Toktar for Acts of Compassion	13
Case 3: The Injustice against Hatice Yıldız for Supporting Her Imprisoned Daughter	15
Case 4: Criminalizing Charity of Salih Muhittin Şahin	17
Case 5: Halit Dumankaya - Allegations of Financing Terrorism Through Corporate Philanthropy	19
Case 6: Targeting of a Healthcare Professionals	20
Case 7: Hasan's Repeated Arrests	20
Case 8: Şeyda's Plight	21
Case 9: Repetitive Detention and Torture of an IT Specialist	22
Case 10: Extensive Arrests in İzmir Targeting Alleged New Gülen Movement Structure	22
Case 11: The Raid and Arrests Involving Concealed Aid Money	23
Case 12: Coordinated Media Coverage of Anti-Hizmet Movement Operation	25
Case 13: Legal Overreach in Detaining Humanitarian Aid Providers	26
Case 14: Targeting Philanthropists under Pretext of Financial Structuring	27
Case 15: Pre-dawn Raid on Philanthropists During Sahur	28
Case 16: Pre-Ramadan Raids on Members of the Gülen Movement	29
Case 17: Massive Detention Wave Despite ECHR Ruling	30
Case 18: Mass Detention of Individuals Assisting Prisoners' Families in Balıkesir	32
Case 19: Adana-based Raid on Philanthropic Activities	32
Case 20: Crackdown on Families of Detainees in Istanbul	33
CONCLUSION: IMPLICATIONS OF SYSTEMATIC SUPPRESSION ON HUMANITARIAN ACTIVITIES	34
Key Observations from Documented Incidents:	34

Executive Summary

This report, issued by the Advocates of Silence Turkey (AST), details an alarming misuse of counterterrorism laws in Turkey to systematically target and dismantle philanthropic efforts supporting the Gülen Movement. It demonstrates how the government's relentless crackdown on these humanitarian activities not only violates basic human rights but also showcases a broader intolerance towards any form of support for the movement. Through detailed analysis of specific cases, this document highlights the severe consequences of these actions, including arbitrary detentions, legal overreach, and the stifling of essential philanthropic work.

Among the numerous cases analyzed, the stories of individuals like Halime Gülsu, Nihat Toktar, Hatice Yıldız, and Halit Dumankaya exemplify the profound personal tragedies behind these statistics. Halime Gülsu, denied essential medical treatment while imprisoned, tragically lost her life, underscoring the dire human cost of these policies. Nihat Toktar, arrested for simply distributing bread to students in need, and Hatice Yıldız, detained for aiding her imprisoned daughter, highlight the indiscriminate targeting of those providing basic humanitarian support. Halit Dumankaya's case, where a respected business leader was imprisoned for alleged affiliations, further illustrates the scope of the crackdown. These stories, along with hundreds of others not detailed in this report, paint a vivid picture of the widespread human cost of this crackdown. Each narrative underscores the devastating impact of Turkey's misuse of counterterrorism measures on ordinary lives, compelling an urgent need for a reconsidered approach that respects human rights and the rule of law.

Key Findings:

- **Misapplication of Justice:** Individuals have been charged under counterterrorism without concrete evidence, relying heavily on affiliations or baseless accusations.
- **Suppression of Philanthropy:** Philanthropic activities, especially those directed towards families affected by government purges, have been criminalized, portraying acts of charity as terrorism.
- **Media and Judicial Bias:** There is significant governmental influence on both media and judiciary, which undermines the objectivity in reporting and adjudicating cases related to the Gülen Movement.
- **Human Rights Violations:** The aggressive enforcement of counterterrorism laws has led to severe human rights violations, including the denial of medical care, inhumane detention

conditions, and unwarranted seizures of property.

This report calls for international attention and intervention with specific recommendations:

1. Establish independent monitoring bodies to oversee Turkey's adherence to international human rights obligations.
2. Urge the Turkish government to revise its counterterrorism laws to ensure they cannot be misused to target humanitarian actions.
3. Encourage international human rights organizations to increase support for individuals and families affected by the crackdown in Turkey.

In conclusion, the systematic targeting of individuals under the guise of counterterrorism not only disrupts lives but also severely impacts Turkey's legal and social fabric, questioning the integrity of its commitment to upholding fundamental human rights and freedoms. The global community must respond, ensuring that humanitarian principles guide our actions and that those facing persecution are not forgotten. This is essential for upholding the dignity and rights of all individuals and for maintaining the social cohesion necessary for any functioning democracy.

Introduction

The Gülen Movement, a global social and religious initiative inspired by the teachings of Fethullah Gülen, has historically been influential in various sectors within Turkey, including education, media, and politics. Once allies, the Turkish government and the Gülen movement experienced a dramatic fallout, particularly visible after the 2013 corruption investigations, which the government saw as an attempt by the movement to overthrow it. This tension culminated in the government accusing the Gülen movement of orchestrating the failed coup attempt on July 15, 2016. Following the coup, the Turkish authorities have targeted the movement in an extensive and ongoing crackdown.

Understanding this crackdown is vital not only because of its scale and intensity but also due to its profound implications on society and the rule of law in Turkey. The actions taken against the Gülen movement have led to severe consequences for thousands of individuals, including job losses, imprisonment, and social ostracization. It is important to note that Turkey has labeled the movement as an armed terrorist organization, opting to refer to it as the Fetullahist Terror Organization (FETÖ) rather than by its original name, the "Hizmet Movement." This renaming is significant, as it deviates from the common practice of addressing organizations, even those designated as terrorist, by their self-identified names. Instead, the government has deliberately chosen a name that casts the movement in a negative light, avoiding the use of its original name which translates to "Service Movement," and carries connotations of benevolence rather than terror.

Objective

Prepared by AST, this report aims to illuminate the extensive and profound implications of the Turkish government's crackdown on the Gülen Movement, emphasizing the humanitarian crises it has engendered. It argues that the measures taken, which range from mass detentions to socio-economic exclusions, amount to a form of social genocide, systematically stripping away the means for thousands of individuals to sustain their lives, including employment, social services, and even humanitarian aid. Through detailed documentation and analysis of individual cases and its classification as a crime to offer aid to affected families, this report seeks to illustrate how these measures effectively condemn individuals to a civil death, stripping them of their rights and dignities without recourse.

Methodology

We utilized various news stories and articles as primary sources to collect information about the nature and consequences of the government's actions. Our methodology also involved directly contacting individuals and families affected by the crackdown, many of whom refused to speak, and those who did chose to remain anonymous due to fear of reprisal. Our analysis will demonstrate that the intensity of the crackdown has not diminished since its inception in 2016. Furthermore, we will explore the motivations behind the Turkish government's refusal to allow even humanitarian aid to those who are in desperate need. Additionally, the report scrutinizes the influence of governmental control over the judiciary and media, which has perpetuated a biased narrative against the Gülen Movement.

The Social Genocide in Numbers

As discussed above, the movement has been systematically stripped of its societal standing and rights, leading some analysts to describe the situation as akin to "social genocide." The term "genocide" was first introduced into global discourse by Raphael Lemkin in 1944 to describe the Nazi persecutions, emphasizing not only the physical annihilation of a people but also the destruction of the cultural and collective identity of the targeted group. Genocide can extend beyond outright killings to include causing serious mental or physical harm, deliberately inflicting conditions calculated to bring about a group's physical destruction, imposing measures intended to prevent births, and forcibly transferring children of the group to another group.

The actions taken by the Turkish government post-July 15, 2016, manifest these broader definitions of genocide, adapted to the context of social and cultural destruction:

- Immediate Legal and Professional Repercussions: The day following the coup attempt saw the dismissal of five members of the High Council of Judges and Prosecutors. Subsequently, 2,745 judges were suspended, including substantial numbers from both administrative and judicial branches.

- Mass Detentions and Dismissals: Over 10,000 individuals were detained within the first week alone. Decree Law No. 668 led to the dismissal of 1,684 military personnel barely 12 days after the coup. The purge expanded to 4,360 judges and prosecutors, including high-ranking members from the Supreme Court and Council of State.

- Institutional Shutdowns and Seizures: The crackdown led to the closure of 1,125 associations, 934 educational institutions, 104 foundations, 35 medical centers, and 15 universities. Additionally, 985 companies were confiscated.

- Widespread Expulsions and Investigations: Within five months of the coup attempt, approximately 80,000 individuals were expelled from the public sector. To date, over 2,217,572 investigation files have been opened regarding alleged affiliations to the movement, leading to more than 500,000 arrests.

Cultural and Social Annihilation

This systematic and targeted policy of cultural and social erasure mirrors some aspects of early measures against Jews in Nazi Germany, where legal, economic, and social rights were systematically stripped away. In Turkey, Hizmet Movement members find themselves redefined as criminals for non-criminal actions, barred from economic participation, and socially ostracized. Such measures have led to what can be termed their "social death," wherein they are effectively excluded from society's economic and social spheres.

This framework of analysis allows for an understanding of the Turkish government's actions as more than a mere response to a failed coup; it represents a concerted effort to eradicate a perceived threat not just physically but socially and culturally. This approach has profound implications for the rule of law and human rights in Turkey, signaling a troubling departure from democratic norms and the principles of justice.

The Crackdown's Reach to Samaritans

As the Turkish government's crackdown on the Hizmet Movement deepened, its scope extended beyond the immediate members of the movement, affecting an even broader spectrum of society. Family members and relatives of those implicated found themselves ensnared in a web of financial and psychological turmoil. The intensification of these adversities was not limited to the adults but tragically permeated to the younger generation, resulting in a disturbing escalation in suicide rates, notably among teenagers linked to the movement. The grief and despair culminating from the incarceration of their parents or relatives and the ensuing stigmatization led to multiple incidents of suicide, reflecting the profound mental health crises provoked by the crackdown.

Amidst this turmoil, a particularly alarming aspect of the crackdown has been its punitive approach toward individuals and organizations attempting to provide humanitarian aid or support to those affected. Families of the detained or dismissed were left in severe financial distress, often struggling to secure basic necessities. In a societal context where these families were increasingly ostracized, the support from external benefactors became a critical lifeline.

However, the government's actions did not stop at the direct victims of the crackdown but extended to those who showed solidarity or aid. Acts of kindness and support were met with suspicion and repression, drawing parallels to authoritarian tactics where even the slightest association with a targeted group could result in severe repercussions. Helping these families, whether through financial support, offering employment, or even social assistance, became a risky endeavor, with several benefactors finding themselves under scrutiny by state authorities.

Legal and Social Implications

This extension of the crackdown to include those providing assistance highlights a disturbing trend towards a more extensive control of society, where the boundaries of the crackdown are continually expanding. It reflects an approach aimed not only at eradicating a perceived threat but also at stifling any acts of dissent or compassion towards the ostracized group. This strategy has involved:

- Arrests and Detentions: Individuals and leaders of charitable organizations who were merely providing humanitarian aid were arrested and charged under broad and ambiguously defined anti-terrorism laws.

- Financial Blockades: Legal measures were taken to freeze bank accounts and impose financial restrictions on NGOs and individuals directly or indirectly involved in supporting affected families, effectively crippling their ability to provide support.

- Social Stigmatization: The social fabric around the families and their supporters was systematically targeted, with community ties being severed by fear and suspicion instigated by state rhetoric and actions.

The targeting of those extending support to the families of the Hizmet Movement not only exacerbates the humanitarian crisis but also poses grave concerns for the rule of law and human rights in Turkey. By punishing altruism and solidarity, the crackdown contravenes fundamental human rights norms and international humanitarian standards, which protect the right to receive and provide humanitarian aid. The actions taken by the state in this context reveal a policy that transcends the suppression of a political adversary to encompass the suppression of basic human compassion and societal resilience. This policy may have long-lasting implications not only for the targeted individuals and their families but for Turkish society as a whole, eroding trust in state institutions and undermining the social cohesion necessary for any functioning democracy.

The following sections will present documented incidents and case studies that exemplify the crackdown's severe impact on the lives of individuals and their families. These narratives underscore the urgent need for international awareness and intervention to uphold human rights and restore the rule of law in Turkey. The report provides not only a record of injustices but also serves as a call to action for global advocates and policymakers to address the ongoing humanitarian crisis.

Silencing Compassion: Systematic Crackdowns on Philanthropic Endeavors

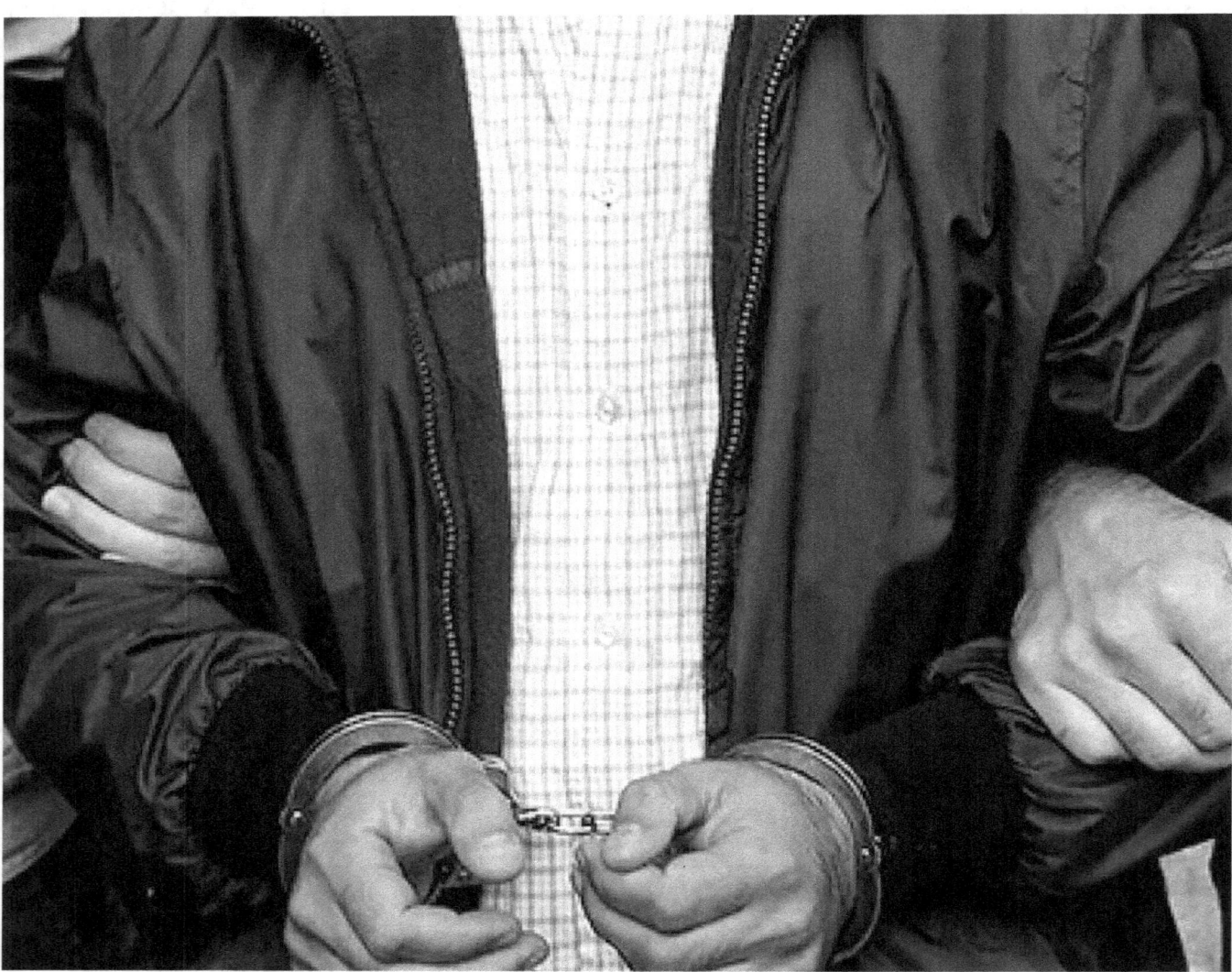

In this section, we attempt to document a series of incidents illustrating the severe governmental measures targeting individuals involved in charitable acts under the guise of national security. Each case herein highlights the increasingly common practice of criminalizing humanitarian aid, where acts of kindness are misconstrued as threats to state stability.

These documented incidents reveal a disturbing pattern: individuals and groups who provide support to marginalized and financially distressed communities—particularly those associated with or sympathetic to the Hizmet Movement—are subjected to raids, detentions, and prosecutions. This pattern not only stifles the fundamental human right to express solidarity and support through philanthropy but also signals a broader assault on civil liberties within the context of an expansive security apparatus.

As you delve into these cases, observe the recurrent themes of disproportionate legal responses to benign activities, the utilization of ambiguous legislation to suppress altruistic efforts, and the profound personal tragedies that unfold when compassion becomes a target of state reprisal. These narratives are not merely accounts of legal battles but are poignant reminders of the human cost of a justice system that increasingly equates benevolence with betrayal.

The methodology employed in this section relies primarily on the collation and analysis of news reports, personal testimonies, and public records. Due to the sensitive nature of the incidents, some sources requested anonymity, necessitating a reliance on altered identities to protect the individuals involved. The disparity in the level of detail among cases is attributable to the varied availability of information; some accounts are deeply personal, offering a window into the emotional and physical toll on those affected, while others are presented in broader strokes, focusing on the aggregate impact and legal implications.

This compilation also acknowledges the inherent media bias and the prevalent narrative framing within the Turkish press, which often portrays members of the Hizmet Movement in a negative light. This vilification campaign not only skews public perception but also complicates the task of drawing a clear and unbiased account of events. It's important to recognize that this selective documentation reflects a broader issue of media freedom and journalistic integrity in Turkey.

Furthermore, the accounts detailed here underscore a critical issue: the instrumentalization of the judiciary and law enforcement as tools to suppress dissent and philanthropic activities under the banner of counterterrorism. This misuse of legal frameworks to criminalize humanitarian aid highlights a troubling erosion of democratic norms and human rights, signaling an urgent need for international scrutiny and advocacy.

By documenting these cases, this report aims to provide a comprehensive overview that captures both the scale of the crackdowns and their deeply personal impacts, thereby contributing to a broader understanding of the ongoing human rights challenges in Turkey.

Case 1: The Tragic Death of Halime Gülsu in Custody

SUMMARY: Halime Gülsu, a young woman detained for her charitable activities in support of families affected by government crackdowns, tragically died in custody due to lack of medical care for her systemic lupus erythematosus. Her arrest was part of a broader operation targeting those affiliated with the Gülen movement, framed under the guise of counterterrorism.[1]

DETAILS: Halime was arrested on February 20, 2018, and initially denied her essential medications for the first 15 days of her detention, which directly contributed to her critical deterioration in health. Despite multiple hospital referrals and medical reports stating her condition was incompatible with prison conditions, she was repeatedly returned to custody, where she eventually succumbed to her illness.

NEGLIGENCE AND LACK OF MEDICAL CARE: The failure to provide necessary medical treatment highlights severe negligence and a disregard for the health and life of prisoners, particularly those with chronic and life-threatening conditions. The handling of her case reflects systemic issues within the penal and judicial systems that fail to uphold basic human rights.

HUMANITARIAN PERSPECTIVE: Halime's activities involved preparing and selling meatballs to raise funds for the families of prisoners, a charitable act criminalized under sweeping anti-terrorism laws.

---

1 Euronews. 2018. Tarsus cezaevindeki hasta tutuklu Halime Gülsu yaşamını yitirdi. [online] Available at: /https://tr.euro/ews.com/2018/04/29/tarsus-cezaevindeki-hasta-tutuklu-halime-gulsu-yasam-n-yitirdi [Accessed 8 May 2024].

Her commitment to helping others, even in the face of personal risk, underscores the humanitarian nature of her actions, starkly contrasting with the allegations of terrorism.

MEDIA AND PUBLIC REACTION: The news of her death sparked outcry on social media and among human rights activists, prompting calls for accountability from the Justice Ministry. However, official responses denied any neglect, stating that her medical needs were met—an assertion contradicted by family and witnesses.

LEGAL AND ETHICAL IMPLICATIONS: The criminalization of humanitarian aid and the subsequent mistreatment of Halime Gülsu in prison spotlight the misuse of anti-terrorism laws against nonviolent activists and the vulnerable. Her case raises significant concerns about the erosion of legal protections and justice, particularly for those opposing or perceived as opposing government policies.

CALL FOR ACCOUNTABILITY AND REFORM: The circumstances of Halime Gülsu's death demand a transparent investigation and hold those responsible accountable. It underscores the urgent need for reforms in the prison healthcare system and the treatment of prisoners, particularly those with serious health conditions. Her case serves as a critical reminder of the human cost of harsh governmental policies and the need for a commitment to human rights and dignity within all sectors of governance.

Case 2: The Persecution of Nihat Toktar for Acts of Compassion

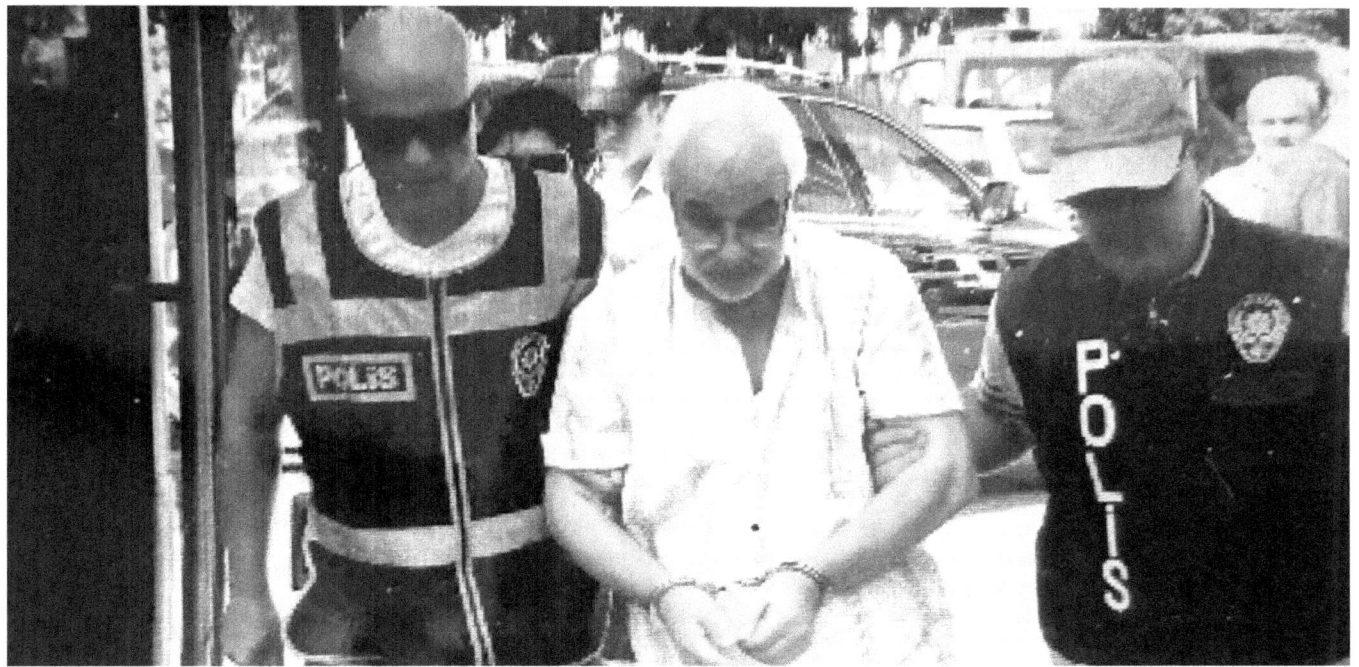

SUMMARY: Nihat Toktar, a 78-year-old former banker and bakery owner, was re-arrested on December 6, 2023, after an appellate court upheld a previous sentence of 6 years and 10 months. The charges stemmed from his alleged connections to the Hizmet Movement, specifically for donating bread to student houses, which was interpreted as support to a group labeled by the government as a terrorist organization.[2]

DETAILS: Nihat Toktar's conviction was heavily based on the testimony of an anonymous witness who claimed knowledge of Toktar's bread donations to student residences. The accusations against him included attending religious gatherings and being part of business networks associated with the Hizmet Movement. Despite his advanced age and serious health issues, including cataracts, prostate problems, and hypertension, his requests for a retrial and postponement of his sentence were denied, raising serious human rights concerns.

HUMANITARIAN AND DRAMATIC ASPECTS: Toktar's case is particularly tragic due to the humanitarian nature of the actions for which he was prosecuted. His commitment to supporting students by providing basic necessities like bread, previously recognized by local officials as commendable, was criminalized in the aftermath of the political crackdown. The dramatic impact of his arrest and the conditions of his detention highlight a disregard for human dignity and the well-being of the elderly in custody.

MEDIA AND LEGAL NARRATIVE: The story of Nihat Toktar, as reported, showcases the harsh measures taken against individuals under broad and ambiguous anti-terrorism laws. The narrative pushed by state-controlled media and echoed across various platforms underscores a concerted effort to vilify and suppress any affiliations with the Hizmet Movement. The dramatic and emotional plea by Toktar's son, who highlighted the inhuman treatment his father received despite his contributions to society, paints a grim picture of the justice system being used as a tool for political repression.

CRITIQUE OF PROSECUTORIAL APPROACH: The legal proceedings against Toktar raise significant concerns about the fairness and impartiality of the judicial process. The reliance on anonymous witnesses and the punitive measures against elderly individuals for non-violent, humanitarian activities point to a misuse of the legal system for political ends. This misuse illustrates a broader pattern of targeting and disenfranchising those associated with the Hizmet Movement, often without substantive evidence linking them to any criminal activities.

---

2   Kronos36. 2024. Fırıncı Nihat amca, öğrenci evlerine ekmek dağıttığı için tekrar tutuklandı. [online] Available at: https://kronos36.news/tr/firinci-nihat-amca-ogrenci-evlerine-ekmek-dagittigi-icin-tekrar-tutuklandi/ [Accessed 7 May 2024].

SOCIETAL AND INTERNATIONAL IMPLICATIONS: The case of Nihat Toktar serves as a stark example of how state mechanisms can be mobilized against citizens, turning acts of kindness into grounds for severe legal punishment. This not only affects the individuals and their families but also sends a chilling message to society about the risks of providing humanitarian aid. The international community's response to such cases is often muted, but they pose serious questions about adherence to universal human rights standards and the rule of law.

Case 3: The Injustice against Hatice Yıldız for Supporting Her Imprisoned Daughter

SUMMARY: Hatice Yıldız, a 75-year-old woman, was taken from her home on a stretcher and incarcerated on March 22, 2024, after being sentenced to 4 years and 2 months in prison for sending 278 Turkish Lira ($9) each to her daughter and three other detainees. This act, which she carried out to support her incarcerated daughter and others in similar dire circumstances, was deemed criminal under broad anti-terrorism laws.[3]

DETAILS: Hatice was convicted for what is fundamentally an act of maternal and humanitarian support. Her health deteriorated significantly in prison, where she has faced multiple health crises

---

[3] Kronos36. 2024. Sedyeyle tutuklanan Hatice teyze hapiste fenalaştı: 'Biz anneler cezaevine gide gele…'. [online] Available at: https://kronos36.news/tr/sedyeyle-tutuklanan-hatice-teyze-hapiste-fenalasti-biz-anneler-cezaevine-gide-gele/ [Accessed 8 May 2024].

without adequate care. This situation highlights the harsh conditions elderly prisoners, especially those arrested under politically motivated charges, have to endure in Turkey.

MEDIA AND NARRATIVE CONTROL: The media coverage of Hatice Yıldız's case by outlets sympathetic to opposition causes starkly contrasts with the silence in state-controlled media, likely to avoid public backlash over the cruel treatment of an elderly, ill woman. This disparity in reporting reflects a controlled narrative that avoids spotlighting the government's harsh treatment of vulnerable populations.

HUMANITARIAN AND EMOTIONAL IMPACT: The details of Hatice's case are deeply troubling. She is a mother trying to support her daughter, who has been in solitary confinement. The emotional and physical toll on Hatice, highlighted by her inability to walk and her serious health issues, underscores the inhumanity of her treatment. The decision to imprison her, especially in such a frail state, illustrates a severe lack of compassion and justice within the judicial system.

LEGAL AND SOCIETAL IMPLICATIONS: The imprisonment of Hatice Yıldız raises significant legal and ethical questions. The use of anti-terrorism laws to imprison a sick, elderly woman for small financial transfers to her daughter showcases the misuse of these laws against non-violent, vulnerable individuals. This not only breaches basic human rights but also damages the credibility of the legal system, which appears to be used as a tool for political repression rather than for upholding justice.

CRITIQUE OF JUDICIAL PROCESS: The reliance on such minor evidence to convict and imprison an elderly woman reflects a judicial process that is heavily influenced by political objectives rather than evidence-based, fair legal practices. Her case is a poignant example of how laws can be interpreted in ways that lead to grave injustices, particularly against those who are least able to defend themselves.

BROADER CONTEXT AND CALL FOR JUSTICE: Hatice Yıldız's story is a stark reminder of the broader issue of human rights abuses under the guise of counterterrorism in Turkey. Her case calls for international scrutiny and domestic reconsideration of the use of anti-terrorism laws, advocating for reforms to protect the rights of all citizens, particularly the most vulnerable. The story of Hatice Yıldız should compel both national and international bodies to reconsider the human cost of such policies and the urgent need for comprehensive judicial reform in Turkey.

Case 4: Criminalizing Charity of Salih Muhittin Şahin

SUMMARY: Salih Muhittin Şahin, a pastry chef from Zonguldak, was indicted for allegedly providing financial support to the families of individuals detained and dismissed under accusations linked to the Gülen movement. This case highlights the broader trend of criminalizing humanitarian acts under the guise of counterterrorism.[4]

DETAILS OF THE ACCUSATIONS: The indictment, prepared by the Zonguldak Prosecutor's Office, alleges that Şahin used a communication program named "Falcon" associated with the Gülen movement. It claims that during house raids, law enforcement found books and digital evidence linked to the organization, and notes containing names and ID numbers of other alleged members. Notably, financial transactions traced back to Şahin included charitable donations to families in need, which were treated as acts of providing financial support to a terrorist organization.

CRITIQUE OF THE LEGAL PROCESS AND MEDIA LANGUAGE: The narrative constructed by the state media, particularly Anadolu Agency, emphasizes the criminal nature of these transactions without acknowledging their charitable context. Terms like "silahlı terör örgütüne üye olma" (membership in an armed terrorist organization) are frequently used to frame charitable actions in a sinister

---

4   Anadolu Agency. 2024. FETÖ sanıklarının ailelerine para yardımı iddianamede. [online] Available at: https://www.aa.com.tr/tr/turkiye/feto-saniklarinin-ailelerine-para-yardimi-iddianamede/1351562 [Accessed 7 May 2024].

light, significantly impacting public perception and further alienating the accused from societal sympathy. Additionally, the reliance on secret witnesses and their testimony, which included vague claims of Şahin seeking individuals in financial need to provide assistance, underscores the absurdity and potential for manipulation within the legal process. This approach not only lacks substantial evidence but also heavily leans on the controversial use of secret testimonies that can neither be verified nor effectively challenged by the defense, highlighting significant flaws in the judicial proceedings.

HUMANITARIAN PERSPECTIVE: The money Şahin is accused of transferring was intended for humanitarian purposes—to assist the families suffering due to the incarceration or job loss of a family member under the broad purges following the 2016 coup attempt. These actions, under different circumstances, would likely be recognized as acts of charity.

ANOMALIES AND PROPAGANDA: The uniformity in the reporting style across various state-controlled and affiliated media outlets, with little to no variation in the narrative or critical examination of the charges, underscores a coordinated effort to justify the government's crackdown on dissent. The absence of balanced reporting, particularly the lack of attention to the humanitarian side of the story, illustrates the use of media as a tool for state propaganda.

LEGAL AND ETHICAL IMPLICATIONS: This case, too, like the others, exemplifies the dangerous precedent of utilizing anti-terrorism laws to criminalize basic human kindness and support systems within society. It raises critical questions about the erosion of legal safeguards and the potential for abuse of law in political purges.

Case 5: Halit Dumankaya - Allegations of Financing Terrorism Through Corporate Philanthropy

SUMMARY: Halit Dumankaya, a prominent construction magnate and one of the executives of Dumankaya Construction, was arrested along with six others under allegations of providing financial support to the Hizmet Movement. The charges against him included financing terrorism and laundering money derived from criminal activities.[5]

DETAILS: On April 18, 2016, a large-scale operation was conducted leading to the detention of 105 individuals, with 44 initially requested for arrest. Dumankaya, aged 76, was among those whose arrest was formalized. During his interrogation, which lasted approximately nine hours, Dumankaya defended himself vigorously. He stated that his company, being one of the top construction firms in Turkey and scrutinized by tax inspectors daily for four years, has always operated within legal bounds. He emphasized his and his family's dedication to the nation, denying any wrongdoing or connection to harmful activities against the state. Dumankaya highlighted that he did not personally know 90% of the scholarship recipients his company supported, underscoring the philanthropic nature of the contributions rather than any intent to support illegal activities.

---

5 Diken. 2024. 'FETÖ/PDY' operasyonunda Dumankaya İnşaat'ın patronu tutuklandı. [online] Available at: https://www.diken.com.tr/fetopdy-operasyonunda-gozaltina-alinan-dumankaya-insaatin-sahibi-tutuklandi/ [Accessed 8 May 2024].

ACCUSATIONS AND DEFENSE: The judiciary claimed that Dumankaya and his co-defendants used their resources to launder money and provide financial support to a terrorist organization. Dumankaya's defense argued that these were regular corporate and charitable activities, misinterpreted as criminal support due to the broad and ambiguous definitions of terrorism in current laws. The arrests, he argued, were part of a wider crackdown on economic freedoms, where even legitimate business activities were being criminalized under the guise of counterterrorism.

HUMANITARIAN IMPACT: The case of Halit Dumankaya illustrates the severe implications of state policies on individuals and businesses, especially those in prominent positions within society. The use of anti-terrorism laws to target business philanthropy disrupts not only the lives of the individuals involved but also the many beneficiaries of their charitable activities. The repercussions extend beyond the immediate legal battles, affecting the broader economic and social fabric of the community.

Case 6: Targeting of a Healthcare Professionals

SUMMARY: Murat, a heart surgeon, was arrested and imprisoned for two years due to alleged connections with the Hizmet Movement. Despite his release and return to medical practice, he and several colleagues were re-arrested for providing medical assistance to families impacted by government purges.[6]

DETAILS: This case highlights the persecution of professionals engaging in compassionate, humanitarian activities that are not recognized as crimes under current laws. Their commitment to aiding the disenfranchised directly contradicts the terrorism charges levied against them, pointing to a misuse of counterterrorism measures to suppress basic human rights and democratic freedoms.

Case 7: Hasan's Repeated Arrests

SUMMARY: Hasan, a 61-year-old small businessman from Central Anatolia, was initially arrested in 2017 and served a year in prison before being conditionally released after receiving a 7.5-year sentence. In 2023, he was re-arrested under the pretext of "restructuring" and spent an additional 4.5 months in jail. The trigger for his surveillance was a visit to a former cellmate's mother, requested by the cellmate who had been extradited back to Turkey under dramatic circumstances.[7]

---

[6] Source: Direct testimony. Details altered for privacy.

[7] Source: Direct testimony. Details altered for privacy.

INITIAL ARREST AND SURVEILLANCE: Hasan's ordeal began when he obliged a former cellmate's request to check on his elderly mother, who believed her son was still abroad. This visit marked the beginning of a year-long physical surveillance that eventually led to Hasan's re-arrest.

CHARGES AND RE-ARREST: His community service activities, including distributing food, coal, and Qurbani (sacrificial meat) during Ramadan, were cited as reasons for his detention along with about 40 others; seven were detained.

JUDICIAL PROCESS: Throughout his 4.5-month re-incarceration, no formal charges were laid nor was an indictment prepared. He was suddenly released without trial but remains under judicial supervision with mandatory weekly check-ins.

SEIZURE OF ASSETS: During his arrest, personal funds and his wife's jewelry were confiscated under accusations of "restructuring."

HUMANITARIAN EFFORTS CRIMINALIZED: Hasan is accused based solely on his philanthropic outreach, evidenced by non-secretive text messages to aid recipients. These activities are inexplicably linked to charges of restructuring.

Case 8: Şeyda's Plight

SUMMARY: Şeyda, a former teacher at the Ministry of National Education (MEB), was dismissed from her job after the July 15 coup attempt due to her membership in a trade union. She tried to make ends meet by making içli köfte, manti, and handicrafts, and supported other families victimized by the State of Emergency decrees (KHK) with food, groceries, and financial aid.[8]

BACKGROUND AND DISMISSAL: Post-coup, Şeyda was dismissed for her union activities, pushing her to support herself through culinary and craft endeavors.

CHARITABLE WORK: She provided financial support from her sales to a woman she met outside a prison, who had an autistic child. This woman, upon being detained, mentioned Şeyda's assistance in her testimony.

SURVEILLANCE AND ARREST: This disclosure led to Şeyda being placed under physical surveillance. Her acts of sending food packages to other victims' families via courier were documented, leading to her arrest.

LEGAL CHALLENGES: Şeyda faced two months of house arrest and her trial continues, with the

8

prosecutor seeking an 8-year sentence for charges related to "new structuring" activities.

PERSONAL STRUGGLES: During this period, her marriage ended in divorce following her husband's complaints to the prosecutor, leaving her to fend for herself and her three children.

Case 9: Repetitive Detention and Torture of an IT Specialist

SUMMARY: Mehmet, an IT specialist, faced repeated detentions: first for his alleged role in the movement, and again for assisting needy families of those purged. His humanitarian efforts were met with torture and denial of legal rights, showcasing a severe breach of human rights under the guise of counterterrorism. [9]

DETAILS: The re-arrest for aiding impoverished families, despite a prior acquittal, underlines the ongoing criminalization of benevolence and the government's broad definition of terrorism. This approach not only infringes on individual freedoms but also perpetrates a form of social genocide by systematically eliminating support networks for the marginalized.

Case 10: Extensive Arrests in İzmir Targeting Alleged New Gülen Movement Structure

SUMMARY: In İzmir, a significant crackdown led to the arrest of 60 individuals under the pretext of dismantling the Gülen Movement's alleged new structure in the Aegean region. This operation, spearheaded by the İzmir Chief Public Prosecutor's Office, is part of a broader series of actions against the movement. [10]

DETAILS: The operation started on July 25, continued with further arrests in İzmir, with additional operations in Istanbul, Muğla, and Aydın. Total of 125 individuals were detained, with 60 arrested. The arrests target those accused of maintaining the organization's structure, collecting funds under the guise of aid, and interacting with imprisoned members, particularly during Ramadan.

CRITIQUE OF LEGAL AND HUMAN RIGHTS IMPLICATIONS: This case exemplifies the ongoing severe measures targeting individuals associated with the Gülen Movement under broad and often ambiguously defined terrorism charges. The actions taken, particularly the large number of arrests

---

9   Source: Direct testimony. Details altered for privacy.

10   TRT Haber. (2023, October 24). "FETÖ'nün yeni yapılanmasına operasyon: 60 tutuklama." Accessed on 8 May 2024. Available at: https://www.trthaber.com/haber/turkiye/fetonun-yeni-yapilanmasina-operasyon-60-tutuklama-328168.html

and the conditions under which these operations are conducted, spotlight the extensive reach of anti-terrorism laws against civic groups and raise urgent concerns about legal rights and the rule of law in Turkey. The scale and nature of the detentions raise significant human rights concerns, highlighting issues of due process and the broad application of anti-terrorism laws.

MEDIA AND PROPAGANDA DYNAMICS: The operations were accompanied by significant media coverage, which often portrays the accused in a manner that presupposes guilt, potentially prejudicing public perception and the fairness of upcoming trials.

Case 11: The Raid and Arrests Involving Concealed Aid Money

SUMMARY: On March 22, 2022, Turkish anti-terrorism police (TEM) conducted raids on 14 addresses in Istanbul and Bursa, arresting 11 individuals under suspicions of affiliation with the Hizmet Movement. During the searches, significant amounts of money and valuables were found hidden in unusual places, including inside a vacuum cleaner, which the media highlighted with a tone of sensationalism.[11]

---

11   Sözcü. (2022, March 31). "FETÖ operasyonunda şaşkına çeviren manzara: Süpürgeden para fışkırdı." Accessed on 8 May 2024. Available at: https://www.sozcu.com.tr/fetonun-guncel-yapilanmasina-6-tutuklama-wp7044776

DETAILS: The operation led to the discovery of 322,180 Turkish Lira, 93,315 US Dollars, 4,485 Euros, gold valued at 483,580 Turkish Lira, and various other valuables including 21 pieces of jewelry and 129 aid cards each loaded with 100 Turkish Lira. The report from Sözcü, a Turkish news outlet, employed a dramatic tone in describing the discovery of money in a vacuum cleaner, framing it as a bizarre and suspicious act. This framing serves to mock and criminalize the efforts of those involved in collecting and distributing aid. The language used by the media in reporting these raids often reflects a subjective bias, contributing to the stigmatization of the Hizmet Movement. Terms like "astonishing scene" and vivid descriptions of the money "bursting" from a vacuum cleaner sensationalize the situation, which can distort public perception and undermine the serious human rights implications of such crackdowns.

HUMANITARIAN CONCERNS AND ACCUSATIONS: The individuals involved were reportedly collecting aid to support needy families and students, a humanitarian act turned perilous under stringent anti-terrorism laws. The fear of being illegitimately charged with terrorism compelled them to take extreme measures to conceal their humanitarian efforts. The use of a vacuum cleaner to hide aid money underscores the desperation and fear among those trying to provide support in a highly surveilled and repressive environment.

LEGAL AND SOCIAL IMPLICATIONS: The arrests and the manner in which the operations were conducted and reported illustrate the broader context of how anti-terrorism laws are being used to suppress basic freedoms and humanitarian activities in Turkey. By criminalizing aid, the state not only infringes on the rights of its citizens but also exacerbates the vulnerabilities of those in need. The portrayal of these activities as clandestine or nefarious by both authorities and certain media outlets further alienates and penalizes those who are already marginalized.

Case 12: Coordinated Media Coverage of Anti-Hizmet Movement Operation

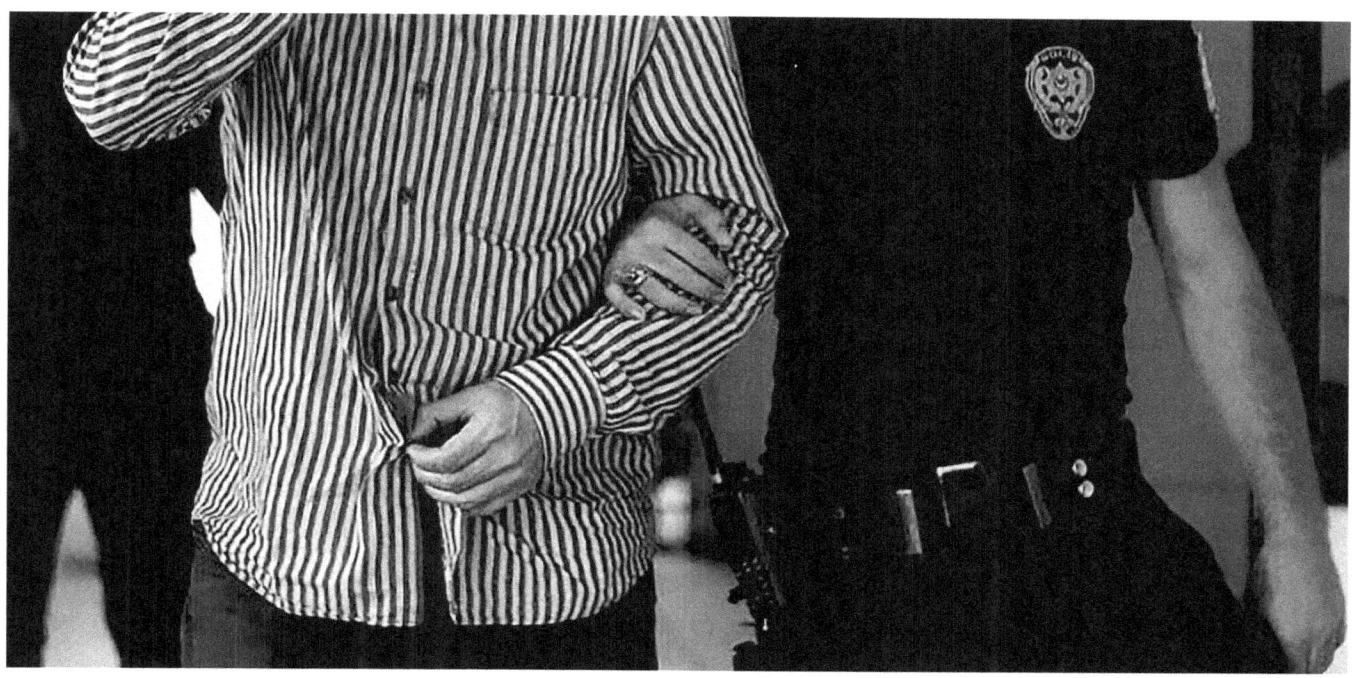

SUMMARY: On April 18, 2024, a nationwide operation titled "Kıskaç-12" was conducted across 14 provinces in Turkey, resulting in the arrest of 60 individuals. The operation, publicly championed by Interior Minister Ali Yerlikaya, seized approximately 6 million TL worth of money, various jewelries, and significant digital materials. This event was widely reported with nearly identical language across multiple media outlets, highlighting a coordinated approach in the portrayal of the Hizmet Movement as a criminal organization.[12]

DETAILS: The operation was described as a significant blow to what the government labels as the FETÖ. The arrested individuals were accused of being part of the organization's "current and secretive military structure", collecting donations under the guise of "himmet" to finance the organization, using secretive houses referred to as "gaybubet houses," and communicating through payphones to avoid detection. The charges also included having definitive prison sentences and search records under ongoing FETÖ investigations.

MEDIA LANGUAGE AND PROPAGANDA: The language used in the reports, particularly phrases like "FETÖ'ye

---

12   ABC Gazetesi. (2024, April 18). "FETÖ'ye Darbe: İçişleri Bakanlığı Operasyonla 60 Şüpheliyi Yakaladi." Accessed on 8 May 2024. Available at: https://abcgazetesi.com/fetoye-darbe-icisleri-bakanligi-operasyonla-60-supheliyi-yakaladi-738586

Darbe" (A Blow to FETÖ) and "Güvenlik güçleri, FETÖ'cülere göz açtırmayacak" (Security forces will not allow FETÖ members any respite), reflects a highly charged, adversarial stance that suggests guilt before a fair trial. This type of language, coupled with the simultaneous release of identical news texts across various platforms, underscores the state's influence over media narratives, which appears to serve a propagandistic purpose rather than objective reporting.

CRITIQUE OF LEGAL AND HUMAN RIGHTS IMPLICATIONS: The accusations levied against the arrested individuals, such as collecting donations or staying in undisclosed residences, are not inherently criminal acts under international law or even under a fair interpretation of Turkish law. These actions, framed as nefarious in state media, are indicative of the broader clampdown on civil liberties under the guise of counterterrorism. The operation's portrayal in the media fails to differentiate between legitimate security concerns and the suppression of humanitarian and social activities, painting all actions with the same broad brush of terrorism.

SOCIETAL IMPACT: The uniformity of the media coverage, the aggressive language used by the Interior Ministry, and the sweeping nature of the arrests all contribute to a climate of fear and suppression targeting not just the individuals involved but also intimidating those who might sympathize with or support the humanitarian aspects of the Hizmet Movement. This approach risks violating basic human rights and further polarizing Turkish society.

Case 13: Legal Overreach in Detaining Humanitarian Aid Providers

SUMMARY: In Istanbul, an operation initiated under allegations of membership in the Gülen Movement led to detention orders for 40 individuals. These individuals were identified for their roles in providing necessary household items and financial support to those unable to pay rent, actions typical of humanitarian aid but criminalized in this context.[13]

DETAILS: The arrests reflect a disturbing misuse of anti-terrorism laws, where benevolent acts are framed as threats to national security. This operation, conducted by the Istanbul Public Prosecutor's Office for Terror and Organized Crime, emphasizes the systemic efforts to suppress any form of support related to the Gülen Movement. By targeting those who merely gathered to provide support through social solidarity, the state demonstrates a significant overreach of legal boundaries and an erosion of democratic freedoms. The legal rationale for these detentions showcases a broader strategy of coercing and isolating individuals associated with the Gülen Movement, thus contributing

---

13   BOLD Medya. (2024, May 7). "İstanbul'da Gülen Hareketi Üyelerine Operasyon: 38 Gözaltı." Accessed on 8 May 2024. Available at: https://www.boldmedya.com/2024/05/07/istanbulda-gulen-hareketi-uyelerine-operasyon-38-gozalti/

to a climate of fear and repression.

IMPLICATIONS: These actions raise critical concerns about the integrity of the legal system and human rights in Turkey. They underscore the transformation of humanitarian assistance into a criminal act, which not only contravenes basic human rights principles but also highlights the government's ongoing strategy to dismantle any perceived opposition. The situation reflects a serious decline in the rule of law, where legal provisions are manipulated to serve political ends rather than justice.

Case 14: Targeting Philanthropists under Pretext of Financial Structuring

SUMMARY: In Ankara, a new round of detentions was orchestrated under the guise of dismantling the Gülen Movement's alleged "current financial structuring". The investigation led to detention orders for 16 philanthropists accused of providing aid to those in need.[14]

DETAILS: This case is part of a broader pattern where individuals offering humanitarian aid are targeted and criminalized. According to the Ankara Public Prosecutor's Office, the arrests were based on the testimonies of repentant suspects, analysis of digital materials, and various surveillance methods. These philanthropists were detained under allegations of membership in the Gülen Movement, highlighting the state's continued efforts to label humanitarian activities as threats to national security.

IMPLICATIONS: The detentions underscore significant issues within the Turkish legal system, where philanthropy is suspiciously linked to terrorism. This approach not only stifles community support and solidarity but also serves as a tactic to instill fear among civil society members. The use of ambiguous and broad charges reflects a judicial strategy that compromises the rule of law and casts a wide net over any acts of kindness, framing them as criminal activities.

---

14   BOLD Medya. (2024, April 22). "Ankara merkezli soruşturmada 16 hayırsevere gözaltı kararı." Accessed on 8 May 2024. Available at: https://www.boldmedya.com/2024/04/22/ankara-merkezli-sorusturmada-16-hayirsevere-gozalti-karari/

Case 15: Pre-dawn Raid on Philanthropists During Sahur

SUMMARY: During sahur (pre-dawn meal during Ramadan), 70 individuals were detained in a nationwide operation across 20 provinces, under allegations of membership in the Gülen Movement. The detainees included notable philanthropists.[15]

ACCUSATIONS: The detained individuals were accused of being members of the Gülen Movement. These arrests were part of a coordinated effort by various branches of the Turkish security apparatus, including the Intelligence Directorate of the National Police and the Anti-Smuggling and Organized Crime Department.

OPERATION DETAILS: The operation was publicly announced by Interior Minister Ali Yerlikaya via social media. It involved simultaneous raids in Aksaray, Bolu, Gaziantep, Sakarya, Muğla, Mersin, Manisa, Istanbul, Kayseri, Kars, Erzurum, İzmir, Elazığ, Adana, Uşak, Denizli, Sivas, Mardin, Edirne, and Bursa. During these raids, personal electronic devices such as phones, tablets, and computers were confiscated.

MEDIA COVERAGE AND GOVERNMENT STATEMENTS: Yerlikaya highlighted the extensive coordination and execution of these operations, stressing the government's ongoing commitment to disrupting the activities of the Gülen Movement.

IMPLICATIONS: This case exemplifies the Turkish government's extensive use of law enforcement agencies to conduct sweeping raids against individuals associated with the Gülen Movement, often under the cover of night or during religiously significant times to maximize impact and perhaps minimize scrutiny. The targeting of individuals known for their philanthropic efforts, especially during a culturally and religiously sensitive period, highlights the broader implications for civil liberties and the rule of law in Turkey. The case raises significant concerns about the proportionality and justification of such measures, which seem to align with broader patterns of suppressing dissent and controlling civil society under the guise of counterterrorism.

---

15   BOLD Medya. (2024, March 29). "Hayırseverlere sahur operasyonu: 70 kişi gözaltına alındı." Accessed on 8 May 2024. Available at: https://www.boldmedya.com/2024/03/29/hayirseverlere-sahur-operasyonu-70-kisi-gozaltina-alindi/

Case 16: Pre-Ramadan Raids on Members of the Gülen Movement

SUMMARY: Just before the month of Ramadan, a large-scale operation was conducted across 30 provinces in Turkey, resulting in the detention of 91 individuals associated with the Gülen Movement. The operation was initiated under allegations of membership in the movement, with the added accusation of providing aid.[16]

ACCUSATIONS: The individuals were accused of aiding through various means, which the government labels as support for a terrorist organization. This broad accusation often encompasses charitable activities and community support, which are criminalized under the current legal framework against the Gülen Movement.

OPERATION DETAILS: Coordinated by the Directorate of Counterterrorism (TEM), Intelligence Directorate, and the Directorate of Anti-Smuggling and Organized Crimes, the operation targeted cities including Istanbul, Ankara, Kocaeli, Aydın, and many others. Interior Minister Ali Yerlikaya announced that substantial amounts of Turkish Lira, digital materials, and organizational documents were seized during the raids. The public statements about the raids highlighted the seizure of funds and documents but

---

16   BOLD Medya. (2024, March 9). "Gülen Hareketi mensuplarına Ramazan öncesi operasyon: Suçlama yardım yapmak." Accessed on 8 May 2024. Available at: https://www.boldmedya.com/2024/03/09/gulen-hareketi-mensuplarina-ramazan-oncesi-operasyon-suclama-yardim-yapmak/

failed to specify the exact reasons for the confiscations or the nature of the so-called organizational documents, raising concerns about the transparency and legality of the process.

IMPLICATIONS: This case is indicative of the ongoing strategy employed by the Turkish government to suppress the Gülen Movement by targeting its members systematically across the country, especially during sensitive times such as just before Ramadan. The raids not only disrupt community and religious preparations but also perpetuate a climate of fear and suppression under the guise of counterterrorism. The vagueness of the charges and the timing of the operations suggest a continued effort to delegitimize and criminalize any affiliations with the movement, thereby impacting basic human rights and freedoms. This approach raises serious questions about the rule of law and the use of state power in personal and community affairs in Turkey.

Case 17: Massive Detention Wave Despite ECHR Ruling

SUMMARY: In a significant raid across Turkey, 611 individuals were detained under the allegation of membership in the Gülen Movement. These detentions occurred despite recent rulings by the European Court of Human Rights (ECHR) indicating that the activities these individuals were involved in—such as opening student houses and aiding families of detainees—do not constitute crimes under European human rights standards.[17]

---

17   BOLD Medya. (2023, October 24). "AİHM kararı ortadayken Gülen Hareketi'ne üyelik iddiasıyla 611 kişi gözaltına alındı." Accessed on 8 May 2024. Available at: https://www.boldmedya.com/2023/10/24/aihm-karari-

ALLEGATIONS: The detained individuals were accused of opening student houses, assisting families of prisoners, and being mentioned in decrypted Bylock content—activities that the ECHR has previously ruled are not sufficient grounds for criminal charges.

ECHR RULING: On September 26, prior to the raids, the ECHR issued the Yalçınkaya decision, highlighting that Turkish judicial proceedings had victimized individuals for actions not considered criminal under Turkish or European law.

SCOPE OF DETENTIONS: The detentions were concentrated in cities like Ankara and İzmir but spanned across the country, affecting 611 individuals. The raids were conducted early in the morning, signaling a coordinated effort to suppress the movement's activities.

GOVERNMENT STANCE: Interior Minister Ali Yerlikaya announced these operations on social media, emphasizing the involvement of national intelligence and police forces. The reasons cited for the arrests were primarily linked to the use of the Bylock messaging app and financial support to the families of those already imprisoned, under the banner of counterterrorism.

IMPLICATIONS: This case underscores a deep-seated issue within the Turkish legal system concerning the interpretation and application of laws in relation to human rights standards. Despite clear guidance from the ECHR, Turkish authorities continue to pursue extensive crackdowns on the Gülen Movement, raising critical concerns about the rule of law, the politicization of justice, and the

---

ortadayken-gulen-hareketine-uyelik-iddiasiyla-611-kisi-gozaltina-alindi/

overall integrity of human rights in Turkey. The mass detentions illustrate not only a disregard for international legal standards but also the pervasive surveillance and control mechanisms targeting a specific group under the guise of national security.

Case 18: Mass Detention of Individuals Assisting Prisoners' Families in Balıkesir

SUMMARY: Following similar incidents in Antalya, 25 individuals were detained in Balıkesir under accusations of providing support to the families of prisoners. These detentions occurred despite the European Court of Human Rights' rulings that such actions do not constitute a crime.[18]

CHARGES: The detainees are accused of financially supporting the families of individuals who are currently incarcerated, purportedly as part of their alleged membership in the Gülen Movement.

CONTEXT: This follows a pattern of arrests that have been criticized for targeting humanitarian assistance rather than any legitimate criminal activity. The European Court of Human Rights has declared that the grounds for these arrests are not legally sustainable.

OPERATION: Conducted by the teams from the Directorate of Anti-Smuggling and Organized Crime at the Balıkesir Police Department, the operation spanned Balıkesir and four other provinces, resulting in the detention of 25 individuals.

IMPLICATIONS: This case, like all the others, reflects ongoing concerns regarding human rights practices in Turkey, especially in relation to the treatment of individuals connected to the Gülen Movement. The detentions raise significant questions about the abuse of legal mechanisms to suppress dissent and humanitarian activities under the guise of national security. Such actions not only contravene international human rights rulings but also highlight the precarious state of legal protections for freedom of association and support within Turkey.

Case 19: Adana-based Raid on Philanthropic Activities

SUMMARY: In Adana and 7 other provinces, 75 individuals were detained on charges related to their membership in the Gülen Movement. The accusations stemmed from their involvement in community support activities such as providing for the needy, opening student houses, engaging

---

18   BOLD Medya. (2023, September 30). "Antalya'dan sonra Balıkesir: Tutuklu ailelerine yardımda bulunan 25 kişi gözaltına alındı." Accessed on 8 May 2024. Available at: https://www.boldmedya.com/2023/09/30/antalyadan-sonra-balikesir-tutuklu-ailelerine-yardimda-bulunan-25-kisi-gozaltina-alindi/

on social media, and attending discussion meetings.[19]

DETAILS: The police operation was initiated early at dawn, targeting those accused of continuing to engage in social gatherings and sharing on social media platforms, which were labeled as criminal activities. The operation emphasized the Turkish authorities' scrutiny over any social media activities related to the Gülen Movement.

NOTEWORTHY INCIDENT: During the operations, it was noted that the pro-government media coverage intentionally avoided documenting the arrest of veiled women. This strategy appears to be a deliberate effort to prevent stirring discontent or sympathy among conservative supporters of the ruling AKP, who may view the arrest of veiled, Muslim women unfavorably. This selective coverage suggests a tactical media manipulation to maintain public support and avoid backlash within conservative segments of the population.

Case 20: Crackdown on Families of Detainees in Istanbul

SUMMARY: Following an operation based in Istanbul and Erzurum, 7 out of 20 individuals detained were arrested under charges of aiding families of people previously arrested under allegations of being part of the Gülen Movement.[20]

DETAILS: The arrests occurred during pre-dawn raids as part of a broader crackdown alleging membership in the Gülen Movement. Those targeted included dismissed public employees, highlighting the continued pressure on individuals connected to detainees.

LEGAL PROCEEDINGS: After completing the police procedures, those arrested were transferred to the judiciary, where 7 were detained, and the remaining were released under judicial control conditions without formal charges being laid out promptly.

---

19 BOLD Media. (2022). Adana'da yardım faaliyetlerini sürdüren 75 kişiye ters kelepçeli operasyon: Gözaltına alınan başörtülü kadınları kaydetmediler. [online] Available at: https://www.boldmedya.com/2022/11/21/adanada-yardim-faaliyetlerini-surduren-75-kisiye-ters-kelepceli-operasyon-gozaltina-alinan-basortulu-kadinlari-kaydetmediler/ [Accessed 8 May 2024].

20 BOLD Media. (2022). Tutuklu ailelerine yardım ettiği iddiasıyla gözaltına alınan 7 kişi tutuklandı. [online] Available at: https://boldmedya.com/2022/04/12/tutuklu-ailelerine-yardim-ettigi-iddiasiyla-gozaltina-alinan-7-kisi-tutuklandi/ [Accessed 8 May 2024].

Conclusion: Implications of Systematic Suppression on Humanitarian Activities

The documented cases above starkly illuminate the extent and nature of systemic actions against members of the Hizmet movement in Turkey. The narratives collectively underscore a troubling trend: the utilization of broad, vaguely defined counterterrorism laws to legitimize severe crackdowns on philanthropic efforts. These laws, which ostensibly aim to safeguard national security, are applied with such breadth and intensity that they often impinge upon basic human rights and undermine the principles of justice.

Key Observations from Documented Incidents:

1. **Legal and Human Rights Violations:** Many individuals have been detained, charged, or convicted without substantive evidence, merely on the basis of association or philanthropic activities. This practice not only contravenes international human rights norms but also highlights a significant deviation from the rule of law.

2. **Government Influence on Judiciary and Media:** The uniformity in the language used across various media outlets, particularly in the portrayal of these cases, raises concerns about the lack of media independence and the potential manipulation of public perception. Moreover, the alignment of judicial actions with government directives suggests a compromised judiciary, more inclined to serve political objectives than to uphold justice and fairness.

3. **Impact on Non-criminal Activities:** The crackdown has particularly targeted those involved in benign activities such as aid distribution, charity, and even social gatherings, framing these acts as threats to national security. This has not only resulted in the unjust incarceration of individuals but has also significantly chilled similar humanitarian efforts.

4. **Broader Implications for Turkish Society:** The aggressive pursuit of those affiliated with the Hizmet movement has created a climate of fear and suspicion that extends far beyond the direct victims. Families are torn apart, careers are destroyed, and the societal fabric is weakened by the erosion of trust and cohesion.

5. **Message to the International Community:** The situation presents a grim picture of Turkey's adherence to democratic values and its obligations under international law. The

apparent misuse of anti-terrorism laws to stifle dissent and civil liberties is a red flag that has, understandably, drawn criticism from various international actors including human rights organizations and foreign governments.

The cumulative effect of these actions is a significant regression in civil liberties and human rights in Turkey. The documented cases serve as a microcosm of a larger, more systemic issue that affects not only the victims and their families but also the standing of Turkey within the global community. As these operations continue, they not only undermine the rule of law but also erode the foundational principles of a democratic society, highlighting a critical need for reassessment and reform of Turkey's policies and practices regarding human rights and counterterrorism.

SUPPORT AST

☑ CREDIT CARD OR DEBIT
silencedturkey.org/donatenow

☑ PAYPAL
paypal.me/ast111

☑ ZELLE
advocatesofsilencedturkey@gmail.com

☑ PATREON
patreon.com/advocatesofsilencedturkey

THANK YOU FOR YOUR DONATIONS

www.ingramcontent.com/pod-product-compliance
Lightning Source LLC
Chambersburg PA
CBHW062207220526
45470CB00009B/2962